Leadership Legacies:
Words to Enlighten, Persuade and Inspire

Leadership Legacies:

Words to Enlighten, Persuade and Inspire

Myles Martel, Ph.D.

Copyright © 2006 by Myles Martel, Ph.D..

Library of Congress Number: 2005907738
ISBN :   Softcover   1-59926-557-5

All rights reserved. No part of this book may be reproduced or transmitted in any form or by any means, electronic or mechanical, including photocopying, recording, or by any information storage and retrieval system, without permission in writing from the copyright owner.

This book was printed in the United States of America.

To order additional copies of this book, contact:
Xlibris Corporation
1-888-795-4274
www.Xlibris.com
Orders@Xlibris.com
30509

CONTENTS

Acknowledgements 9

Introduction 11

Chapter 1: Leveraging Ronald Reagan's Leadership Lesson:
Defining and Declaring Your Leadership Principles 13

Chapter 2: Leadership 21

Chapter 3: Achievement 31

Chapter 4: Change 35

Chapter 5: Character 41

Chapter 6: Courage 49

Chapter 7: Empowerment 57

Chapter 8: Goodwill 63

Chapter 9: Persuasion & Influence 67

Chapter 10: Preparedness 73

Chapter 11: Self-Awareness & Self-Respect 77

Chapter 12: Teamwork 83

Chapter 13: Vision 87

Special Appreciation 93

Dedication

To the leaders we at Martel and Associates have been privileged to advise, to those who have introduced them to us, and to the members of our firm who have served them so ably.

Acknowledgements

To my wife Leslie whose steady support fueled my desire to write this. To Deborah Deam who ably and cheerfully supported every aspect of this work. To Bob Weiss, David Martel, Gaylon White and Jim Deam who gave me insightful editorial guidance. To Kevin McElgunn, Jeff Dudley and Rob Spurling for providing examples for Chapter One. To Jay Rosales of Xlibris who helped turn all of these collected thoughts into this book. To Lucy my "dogter" whose barks are not quotable, but whose leadership skills are enviable.

Introduction

This book has its roots in a meeting I had with Ronald Reagan 25 years ago. He and I were having a private lunch on the patio of the estate where he and his wife Nancy were living outside Middleburg, Virginia, an impressive property overlooking a captivating vista of the Blue Ridge Mountains. I was there to serve as his personal debate advisor, a role I had assumed following his presidential nomination in 1980.

During our discussion, Reagan, in his inimitably casual, convincing style, stressed how important it was for a leader to be clear to his followers about what he stood for, including how important it was for a leader to reinforce his leadership principles. That insight, exemplified throughout Ronald Reagan's public life, has become a core leadership lesson I have given to hundreds of CEO's and other leaders in business and government during my 25 years as a leadership communication advisor.

This book, in effect a collection of leadership legacies of Ronald Reagan and other prominent figures in business, government, the military, the arts, athletics, the academic world and religion, is aimed to help leaders better understand and articulate their leadership philosophies and the principles that underpin them.

The following chapter provides guidance for framing a leadership credo, that is, a personalized statement of the leader's leadership philosophy and principles.

The quotations which constitute the lion's share of this book have been collected by me for over thirty years. The topics were selected based on the frequency with which they have surfaced in discussions with the leaders we advise. Each quotation is intended to help the leader conceive his or her credo as well as capture aptly, crisply and impressively a point he or she might want to make during a speech or presentation.

May this book help you advance your leadership as you enlighten, persuade and inspire.

Sincerely,

Myles Martel
Gulfstream, Florida
2005

Chapter 1

Leveraging Ronald Reagan's Leadership Lesson: Defining and Declaring Your Leadership Principles

Leveraging Ronald Reagan's Leadership Lesson: Defining and Declaring Your Leadership Principles

Ronald Reagan's leadership lesson was based on the premise that while most of us give at least some credence to the axiom "actions speak louder than words," at times a leader cannot wait for or rely solely on his actions to speak for him, regardless of how communicative they might be. Sometimes the leader recognizes through intuition, input, or both, that people who count on him for leadership expect greater clarity regarding his values, leadership principles, ideas and vision. Moments like these are seized upon throughout history by presidents, governors and civic leaders as they set their agendas and tone through inaugural addresses and other public pronouncements. However, such leadership opportunities have been significantly squandered in the corporate world.

Our experience at Martel & Associates in advising leaders has helped us identify several key reasons why too few of them emulate the practices established in the political realm. They include:

- The leader's lack of clarity regarding his or her leadership philosophy and principles
- Lack of a well-defined leadership culture within the organization which is conducive to such practices
- Lack of appreciation for the potentially positive influence such communication can yield
- Reliance on a command-and-control culture where communication is based on a conservative "need to know" mindset
- An innate unwillingness by the leader to communicate, possibly rooted in introversion, speech anxiety, or some other factor
- Concern that such communication could be perceived as posturing

Our leadership counsel is based on the premise that a leader's philosophy and principles can be better conveyed through explicit communication than by chance or inference. Not being explicit increases the chances that what the leader represents could result in misunderstanding, damaging rumor, and a perception of weak leadership.

Why create and communicate a "Credo"?

The term "Credo" captures well the leadership stance—the philosophy and principles—we advise leaders to craft, articulate and reinforce. Our major reasons for this counsel follow:

- To foster added self-understanding regarding what animates them as leaders
- To publicly express personal accountability for the principles contained in the credo
- To advance alignment with their leadership philosophy
- To advance alignment with those organizational goals related to the credo
- To reinforce and advance the organization's leadership culture

The credo exercise does not call for a boilerplate listing of values, e.g., integrity, teamwork, excellence. Rather, crafting a credo calls for the leader to engage in honest, reflective self examination and articulate a personalized, potentially meaningful—and motivational—set of principles that help describe what animates him as a leader as well as what he expects from his followers.

Self-awareness, therefore, is the bedrock of a credo. Indeed, the greater one's self-awareness, the greater the chances that the credo will be thoughtful, credible and effective. The credo, therefore, should be an authentic representation of who the leader is, what he believes in and what he aspires to be.

Leaders we advise are encouraged to rely on the following sources as they formulate their credos:

- Self-understanding, including intuition
- Formal and informal feedback
- Readings about leadership, including the quotations contained in this book
- Biographies of leaders
- Credos prepared by others they respect

The Power of a Personalized Preamble

The foundation of a leader's credo principles should be a personalized preamble that captures his leadership philosophy. A fine example of a preamble prepared by a leader in our program follows:

> Leaders have the courage to take action when those around them hesitate. Effective leaders energize and influence others in order to achieve significant results. Truly great leaders do all this and more—they create new leaders.
>
> I believe true leadership is the highest form of service. Service to self, service to others, and service to the goals and higher purposes we set before us. I aspire to be a truly great leader in the pursuit of fulfilling my own personal purpose—to lead a life centered on excellence, integrity and faith in God, continuously learning and growing, helping others fulfill their potential.
>
> The following are the leadership principles in which I believe. They are the commitment I make to myself and to those around me.

Principles to Support the Preamble

This alphabetical list of leadership themes represents the major focal points for the principles developed by the leaders we advise. Each principle usually takes the form of a concise pledge or commitment statement, including, on occasion, a development need, such as listening better, being more clear in setting expectations, or handling conflict more effectively. Usually, a leader crafts between 5 and 10 personalized principles selected from these themes:

Accountability	Leadership Culture
Attitude	Leading by Example
Clear Expectations	Learning
Collaboration	Listening
Commitment	Mentoring / Teaching
Communication	Openness
Conflict (constructive vs. destructive)	Optimism
Customer Orientation	Patience

Decision-making	Personal Development
Dialogue and Debate	Quality
Diversity	Resilience
Empowerment	Respect
Engagement	Results orientation
Excellence	Risk tolerance
Feedback	Servant Leadership
Fun	Teamwork
Inclusion	Trust
Integrity	Work-Life Balance

These examples from leaders we have advised illustrate how some of the themes listed above become articulated as credo principles:

Excellence

"Mediocrity is the father of failure; excellence is non-negotiable."

Engagement

"You either want to be successful or you don't. There is no place on the team for those who are not interested in giving their all in order to succeed. I expect total engagement in successfully accomplishing our vision."

Listening

"If I don't listen well, I will neither learn nor lead well; tell me if and when I do not live up to what you expect from me as a listener."

POSITIONING THE CREDO

How and when leaders choose to unveil their credos requires careful thought. Proper positioning and timing of the credo should prevent two potentially counterproductive questions from stakeholders: 1. "Why is he doing this?" 2.

"Why is he doing this now?" Leaders we advise rely mainly on the six positioning strategies reflected in the following examples: Each can be used in a presentation, informal meeting, in writing, or in some combination:

1. Corporate Culture

   "As you know, our CEO has stressed that our collective potential depends on our ability to influence a 'culture of leadership' throughout our organization. Based on this, I chose to define for you what I expect of myself as a leader and what I expect from you through my leadership."

2. Anniversary

   "It has been one year since I assumed this position, and I've decided to share with you my perspective, priorities as well as the leadership principles I will emphasize as we embark on this new year."

3. Leadership Development Program

   "I have been selected by senior management to participate in a leadership development program. One of the exercises in this program is to articulate what I stand for as a leader. I have been encouraged to share these principles with you, and decided that doing so could be beneficial to us both."

4. A Leadership Principle

   "I don't feel it is fair to keep people guessing regarding what a leader stands for. In fact, taken to the extreme, this kind of behavior can be unnecessarily intimidating. For this reason, I've decided to help you better understand those leadership principles which are most important to me and potentially important to you."

5. Crises

   "We have been through a lot lately, and it occurred to me that this would be an appropriate time for me to reflect and share with you what leadership lessons we can glean from this experience and what leadership principles I intend to emphasize to help us advance."

6. Major Organizational Change

"Effective leadership is key to our reorganization plan working. Here are some of the major principles I regard as critical to our success."

We recommend that leaders make their best effort to unveil their credo in person, although geographical distance between the leader and his constituents might pose complications. The leader should be neither defensive nor apologetic in presenting it. A discussion of the credo, in fact, should be initiated confidently, stating the opportunity it represents to those expected to embrace it.

Anchoring the Principles

How a leader communicates his credo for lasting resonance—"anchors" it in the minds of those he seeks to influence—also requires careful thought. Often, leaders are likely to benefit from creating a communication plan to reinforce the credo over time. Thoughtful answers to these questions should help result in an effective plan:

- What venue (or venues) will be best suited to unveiling the credo?
- Should other members of the team be expected to espouse the credo, or one or more of its principles? If so, how?
- Should the credo or any of its principles be reinforced during meetings with the leadership team and through reports?
- Would it be helpful to collect and announce in meetings or by other means, exemplary performance based on credo-related principles?
- Should examples of behavior not consistent with the credo principles be highlighted? If so, how should this be communicated?
- Should the credo principles be incorporated into the performance review process?

As leaders consider these questions, they should strive to ensure that his plan is regarded as credible and practical. When in doubt, the leader should take a conservative approach to the communication plan, seeking reliable, timely feedback throughout the entire process.

In the Final Analysis

Carefully conceived, well-articulated and effectively reinforced, a credo can only bring positive results. The credo should advance a leader's agenda and enhance his self-awareness, clarity, accountability and credibility. Further, it could become one of his leadership legacies, inspiring other leaders in the organization to create their own credos.

Chapter 2

Leadership

Leadership

If your actions inspire others to dream more, learn more, do more and become more, you are a leader.

John Quincy Adams

People judge a leader less by how he or she is doing than by how they are doing.

Anonymous

The first task of a leader is to keep hope alive.

Joe Batten

The manager asks how and when; the leader asks what and why.

Warren Bennis

A potential leader can hardly afford to wait to become a legend in his own time; to satisfy us, he must almost become a legend ahead of his time.

Brock Brewer

The task of leadership is not to put greatness into humanity, but to elicit it, for the greatness is already there.

John Buchan

Leadership is fired in the forge of ambition and opportunity.

James MacGregor Burns

A leader takes people where they want to go. A great leader takes people where they don't necessarily want to go but ought to be.

Rosalynn Carter

I was only the servant of my country and had I, at any moment, failed to express her unflinching resolve to fight and conquer, I should at once have been rightly cast aside.

Winston Churchill

Leaders who win the respect of others are the ones who deliver more than they promise, not the ones who promise more than they can deliver.

Mark Clement

Perhaps the most central characteristic of authentic leadership is the relinquishing of the impulse to dominate others.

David Cooper

Management works in the system; leadership works on the system.

Stephen Covey

Leadership is generally defined as the capacity to make things happen that would otherwise not happen.

Thomas E. Cronin

One cannot govern with 'buts'.

Charles De Gaulle

Every man of action has a strong dose of egotism, pride, hardness, and cunning. But all those things will be forgiven him, indeed, they will be regarded as high qualities, if he can make them the means to achieve great ends.

Charles De Gaulle

I must follow the people. Am I not their leader?

Benjamin Disraeli

The first responsibility of a leader is to define reality. The last is to say thank you. In between the two, the leader must become a servant and a debtor. That sums up the progress of an artful leader.

Max DuPree

We should take care not to make intellect our god. It has, of course, powerful muscles, but no personality. It cannot lead, it can only serve.

Albert Einstein

You do not lead by hitting people over the head—that's assault, not leadership.

Dwight D. Eisenhower

Leadership is the art of getting someone else to do something you want done because he wants to do it.

Dwight D. Eisenhower

Pull the string, and it will follow wherever you wish. Push it, and it will go nowhere.

Dwight D. Eisenhower

Leadership is particularly necessary to ensure ready acceptance of the unfamiliar and that which is contrary to tradition.

Cyril Falls

Leadership is the special quality which enables people to stand up and pull the rest of us over the horizon.

James L. Fisher

How wonderful it is that nobody need wait a single moment before starting to improve the world.

Anne Frank

The trust of the people in the leaders reflects the confidence of the leaders in the people.

Paulo Freire

One of the tests of leadership is the ability to recognize a problem before it becomes an emergency.

Arnold H. Glasgow

A good leader takes a little more than his share of the blame, a little less than his share of the credit.

Arnold H. Glasgow

No creature can fly with just one wing. Gifted leadership occurs where heart and head—feeling and thought—meet. These are the two wings that allow the leader to soar.

Daniel Goleman, Richard Boyatzis, Annie McKee

Most companies don't die because they are wrong; most die because they don't commit themselves . . . You have to have a strong leader setting a direction. And it doesn't even have to be the best direction—just a strong, clear one.

Andy Grove

Leaders are visionaries with a poorly developed sense of fear and no concept of the odds against them.

Robert Jarvik

You can judge a leader by the size of the problem he tackles . . . Other people can cope with the waves, it's his job to watch the tide.

Anthony Jay

The convictions that leaders have formed before reaching high office are the intellectual capital they will consume as long as they continue in office. There is little time for leaders to reflect. They are locked in an endless battle in which the urgent constantly gains on the important.

Henry Kissinger

The great leaders are like the best conductors—they reach beyond the notes to reach the magic in the players.

Blaine Lee

The final test of a leader is that he leaves behind him in other men the conviction and the will to carry on.

Walter Lippman

A leader is the steward of the spirit of his people.

Myles Martel

The debate as to whether or not leaders are born or made is worn and useless. Everyone has the potential to lead in some way. A leader's role is to help his or her people discover and develop that potential.

Myles Martel

A leader draws strength from the people's view that, regardless of circumstance, he or she can help make things better.

Myles Martel

A leader's mindset must be dominated by a bias that favors well grounded possibility over reflexive doubt.

Myles Martel

Perfect leadership is not only elusive, it is impossible. Therefore, regardless of talent or circumstance, one's potential to grow as a leader is virtually unlimited.

Myles Martel

Only one man in a thousand is a leader of men—the other 999 follow women.

Groucho Marx

Leaders must be close enough to relate to others, but far enough ahead to motivate them.

John Maxwell

A leader is one who knows the way, goes the way and shows the way.

John Maxwell

A big man is one who makes us feel bigger when we are with him.

John Maxwell

Leadership is action, not position.

Donald H. McGannon

The real leader has no need to lead—he is content to point the way.

Henry Miller

The final test of a leader is the feeling you have when you leave his presence after a conference or interview. Have you a feeling of uplift and confidence? Are you clear as to what is to be done, and what is your part of the task? Are you determined to pull your weight in achieving the object? Or is your feeling the reverse?

Bernard Law Montgomery

Leadership involves finding a parade and getting in front of it.

John Naisbitt

A leader is a dealer in hope.

Napoleon

Lead me, follow me, or get out of my way.

General George S. Patton

Inventories can be managed, but people must be led.

H. Ross Perot

A competent leader can get efficient service from poor troops, while on the contrary an incapable leader can demoralize the best of troops.

General John J. Pershing

You take people as far as they will go, not as far as you would like them to go.

Jeannette Rankin

You cannot be a leader, and ask other people to follow you, unless you know how to follow, too.

Sam Rayburn

Leaders are people we as followers want to regard with awe as the fullest flowering of our own possibilities.

Gail Sheehy

There are no bad regiments, there are only bad officers.

Field Marshall Lord Slim

In the place where there is a leader, do not seek to become a leader. In the place where there is no leader, strive to become a leader.

Talmud

Do not wait for leaders. Do it alone, person to person.

Mother Teresa

Remember that it is far better to follow than to lead indifferently.

John G. Vance

The only safe ship in a storm is leadership.

Faye Wattleton

Making initiatives successful is all about focus and passionate commitment. The drumbeat must be relentless. Every leadership action must demonstrate total commitment to the initiative.

Jack Welch

Leadership is, among other things, the ability to inflict pain and get away with it—short-term pain for long-term gain.

George F. Will

Leadership—mobilization toward a common goal.

Garry Wills

Absolute identity with one's cause is the first and great condition of successful leadership.

Woodrow Wilson

I do not believe that any man can lead who does not act . . . under the impulse of a profound sympathy with those whom he leads.

Woodrow Wilson

A man is not as big as his belief in himself; he is as big as the number of persons who believe in him.

Woodrow Wilson

Knowledge alone is not enough to get desired results. You must have the more elusive ability to teach and to motivate. This defines a leader; if you can't teach and you can't motivate, you can't lead.

John Wooden

Chapter 3

Achievement

ACHIEVEMENT

The six basic mistakes of man are:

1. The delusion that individual advancement is made by crushing others.
2. The tendency to worry about things than cannot be changed or corrected.
3. Insisting that a thing is impossible because *we* cannot accomplish it.
4. Refusing to set aside trivial preferences.
5. Neglecting development and refinement of the mind and not acquiring the habit of reading and study.
6. Attempting to compel other persons to believe as we do.

Cicero

You will find the key to success under the alarm clock.

Benjamin Franklin

There are no great people in this world, only great challenges which ordinary people rise to meet.

Admiral William Frederick Halsey, Jr.

We are continually faced by great opportunities brilliantly disguised as insoluble problems.

Lee Iacocca

The pessimist sees the difficulty in every opportunity; the optimist, the opportunity in every difficulty.

L.P. Jacks

Champions keep playing until they get it right.

Billy Jean King

Every man feels instinctively that all the beautiful sentiments in the world weigh less than a single lovely action.

James Russell Lowell

For of all sad words of tongue or pen, the saddest are these: "It might have been!"

John Greenleaf Whittier

Chapter 4

Change

CHANGE

There can be change without progress, but not progress without change.

Anonymous

The people who are crazy enough to think they can change the world are the ones who do.

Apple Computer, Inc. (Television ad, CNN, December 15, 2997)

Not everything that is faced can be changed. But nothing can be changed until it is faced.

James Baldwin

When you're through changing, you're through.

Bruce Barton

A new leader has to be able to change an organization that is dreamless, soulless and visionless . . . someone's got to make a wake up call.

Warren Bennis

Never underestimate your power to change yourself; never overestimate your power to change others.

H. Jackson Brown, Jr.

If you don't like the way the world is, you change it. You have an obligation to change it.

Marian Wright Edelman

Be the change you want to see in the world.

Mahatma Gandhi

The prime condition of national survival has been timely adaptation to changing conditions.

B.H. Liddell Hart

All things are in motion and nothing is at rest . . . You cannot go into the same [river] twice.

Heraclitus

Change is not made without inconvenience, even from worse to better.

Richard Hooker

Change is the law of life and those who look only to the past or present are certain to miss the future.

John F. Kennedy

Great change dominates the world, and unless we move with change we will become its victims.

Robert F. Kennedy

The world hates change, yet it is the only thing that has brought progress.

Charles F. Kettering

Never doubt that a small group of thoughtful, concerned citizens can change the world. Indeed it is the only thing that ever has.

Margaret Mead

It is not possible for any thinking person to live in such a society as our own without wanting to change it.

George Orwell

Even if you're on the right track, you'll get run over if you just sit there.

Will Rogers

If you don't like change, you're going to like irrelevance even less.

General Eric Shinseki

Nothing ever is, but all things are becoming . . . all things are the offspring of flux and motion.

Socrates

There are three kinds of people: Those who make things happen, those who watch things happen, and those who ask, "What happened?"

Casey Stengel

All change is a miracle to contemplate; but it is a miracle which is taking place every instant.

Henry David Thoreau

Change is the process by which the future invades our lives.

Alvin Toffler

Whenever an individual or a business decides that success has been attained, progress stops.

Thomas J. Watson

An individual is more apt to change, perhaps, than all the world around him.

Daniel Webster

Consistency is the last refuge of the unimaginative.

Oscar Wilde

If you want to make enemies, try to change something.

Woodrow Wilson

Chapter 5

Character

CHARACTER

He who has never learned to obey cannot be a good commander.

Aristotle

The great hope of society is individual character.

William Ellery Channing

The price of greatness is responsibility.

Winston Churchill

A chief is a man who assumes responsibility. He says, 'I was beaten'; he does not say, 'My men were beaten.'

Antoine De Saint-Exupery

Whoever is careless with the truth in small matters cannot be trusted with the important matters.

Albert Einstein

Try not to become a man of success but rather try to become a man of value.

Albert Einstein

The louder he talked of his honor, the faster we counted our spoons.

Ralph Waldo Emerson

No change of circumstances can repair a defect of character.

Ralph Waldo Emerson

He that is good at making excuses is seldom good at anything else.

Benjamin Franklin

It is a grand mistake to think of being great without goodness; and I pronounce it as certain that there was never yet a truly great man that was not at the same time truly virtuous.

Benjamin Franklin

My rule, in which I have always found satisfaction, is never to turn aside in public affairs through views of private interest; but to go straight forward in doing what appears to me right at the time, leaving the consequences with Providence.

Benjamin Franklin

When wealth is lost, nothing is lost; when health is lost, something is lost; when character is lost, all is lost.

German Proverb

There are many qualities that make a great leader. But having strong beliefs, being able to stick with them through popular and unpopular times, is the most important characteristic of a great leader.

Rudolph W. Giuliani

Fame is a vapor, popularity an accident, riches take wings, those who cheer today will curse tomorrow; only one thing endures—character.

Horace Greeley

Those who stand for nothing fall for anything.

Alexander Hamilton

The man who complains about the way the ball bounces is likely the one who dropped it.

Lou Holtz

The reputation of a thousand years may be determined by the conduct of one hour.

Japanese Proverb

In matters of style, swim with the current; in matters of principle, stand like a rock.

Thomas Jefferson

God grant that men of principle shall be our principal men.

Thomas Jefferson

A man's character is determined by how hard he fights for what he believes in.

Aben Kandel and Warren Duff

The time is always right to do what is right.

Martin Luther King, Jr.

If a man hasn't found anything for die for, he isn't fit to live.

Martin Luther King, Jr.

The quality of a leader is reflected in the standards they set for themselves.

Ray Kroc

Leadership consists not in degrees of technique but in traits of character; it requires moral rather than athletic or intellectual effort, and it imposes on both leader and follower alike the burdens of self-restraint.

Lewis H. Lapham

The fate of a people depends much more on their character than on their intelligence.

Gustave Le Bon

Character is like a tree and reputation like its shadow. The shadow is what we think of it; the tree is the real thing.

Abraham Lincoln

Nearly all men can stand adversity, but if you want to test a man's character, give him power.

Abraham Lincoln

I desire so to conduct the affairs of this administration that if at the end, when I come to lay down the reins of power, I have lost every friend on earth, I shall at least have one friend left, and that friend shall be down inside me.

Abraham Lincoln

Let the people know the truth and the country is safe.

Abraham Lincoln

It's easy to have faith in yourself, and have discipline when you're a winner, when you're number one. What you got to have is faith and discipline when you're not a winner.

Vince Lombardi

Nobody grows old by merely living a number if years. People grow old only by deserting their ideals. Years may wrinkle the skin, but to give up interest wrinkles the soul.

General Douglas MacArthur

The measure of a man's real character is what he would do if he knew he would never be found out.

Thomas Babington Macaulay

When in doubt about honesty, trustfulness, and other moral qualities [of the candidate for a leadership position], a good test is to say to oneself, "Would I go in the jungle with that man?"

Bernard Law Montgomery

Character is what you are in the dark.

Dwight L. Moody

Character is much easier kept than recovered.

Thomas Paine

Physical bravery is an animal instinct; moral bravery is a much higher and truer courage.

Wendell Phillips

Trust is the essence of leadership.

Colin Powell

It is not fair to ask of others what you are unwilling to do yourself.

Eleanor Roosevelt

We may make mistakes—but they must never be mistakes which result from faintness of heart or abandonment of moral principle.

Franklin D. Roosevelt

It is character that counts in a nation as in a man. It is a good thing to have a keen, fine intellectual development in a nation, to produce orators, artists, successful businessmen; but it is an infinitely greater thing to have those solid qualities which we group together under the name of character: sobriety, steadfastness, the sense of obligation toward one's neighbor and one's God, hard common sense, and, combined with it, the lift of generous enthusiasm toward whatever is right.

These are the qualities which go to make up true national greatness.

Theodore Roosevelt

Leadership is a combination of strategy and character. If you must be without one, be without the strategy.

General H. Norman Schwarzkopf

The secret of a leader lies in the tests he has faced over the whole course of his life and the habit of action he develops in meeting those tests.

Gail Sheehy

When you teach your son, you teach your son's son.

The Talmud

Always do right. It will gratify some people and astonish the rest.

Mark Twain

The best index to a person's character is (a) how he treats people who can't do him any good, and (b) how he treats people who can't fight back.

Abigail Van Buren

Leadership is doing what is right when no one is watching.

George Van Valkenburg

I suggest that if you have someone who has negative energy, ask them to join a group with negative energy.... Get the bums out of there.

Jack Welch

Chapter 6

Courage

Courage

Leaders are called to stand in that lonely place between the no longer and the not yet and intentionally make decisions that will bind, forge, move and create history.

we are not called to be popular,
we are not called to be safe,
we are not called to follow,
we are the ones called to take risks,
we are the ones called to change attitudes,
to risk displeasures,
we are the ones called to gamble our lives,
for a better world.

Mary Lou Anderson

Courage is what it takes to stand up and speak; courage is also what it takes to sit down and listen.

Anonymous

Cautious, careful people, always casting about to preserve their reputation and social standing, never can bring about a reform. Those who are really in earnest must be willing to be anything or nothing in the world's estimation, and publicly and privately, in season and out, avow their sympathy with despised and persecuted ideas and their advocates, and bear the consequences.

Susan B. Anthony

The art of leadership is saying no, not yes. It is very easy to say yes.

Tony Blair

A leader must have the courage to act against an expert's advice.

James Callaghan

Most of the important things in the world have been accomplished by people who have kept on trying when there seemed no help at all.

Dale Carnegie

Success is the ability to go from failure to failure without losing your enthusiasm.

Winston Churchill

If you're going through hell, keep going.

Winston Churchill

Abraham Lincoln did not go to Gettysburg having commissioned a poll to find out what would sell in Gettysburg. There were no people with percentages for him, cautioning him about this group or that group or what they found in exit polls a year earlier. When will we have the courage of Lincoln?

Robert Coles

Our greatest glory is not in never falling, but in rising every time we fall.

Confucius

Only those who will risk going too far can possibly find out how far one can go.

T.S. Eliot

Never confuse a single defeat with a final defeat.

F. Scott Fitzgerald

The men who have done big things are those who were not afraid to attempt big things, who were not afraid to risk failure in order to gain success.

B.C. Forbes

All of the great leaders have had one characteristic in common: it was the willingness to confront unequivocally the major anxiety of their people in their time. This, and not much else, is the essence of leadership.

John Kenneth Galbraith

Don't be afraid to take a big step when one is indicated. You can't cross a chasm in two small steps.

David Lloyd George

Companies that create the future are rebels. They're subversives. They break the rules. They're filled with people who take the other side of an issue just to spark a debate. In fact, they're probably filled with people who didn't mind being sent to the principal's office once in a while.

Gary Hamel and C.K. Prahalad

It is not the mountain we conquer but ourselves.

Sir Edmund Hillary

The greatest mistake you can make is to be continually fearing that you'll make one.

Elbert Hubbard

One man with courage makes a majority.

Andrew Jackson

Too many people let others stand in their way and don't go back for one more try.

Rosabeth Moss Kanter

There are risks and costs to a program of action, but they are less than the long-range risks and costs of comfortable inaction.

John F. Kennedy

For without belittling the courage with which men have died, we should not forget those acts of courage with which men . . . have lived.

John F. Kennedy

Only those who dare to fail greatly can ever achieve greatly.

Robert F. Kennedy

The ultimate measure of a man is not where he stands in moments of comfort and convenience, but where he stands at times of challenge and controversy.

Martin Luther King, Jr.

A leader does not deserve the name unless he is willing occasionally to stand alone.

Henry Kissinger

A man who wants to lead the orchestra must turn his back on the crowd.

Max Lucado

Where the willingness is great, the difficulties cannot be great.

Nicolo Machiavelli

Often the difference between a successful man and a failure is not one's better abilities or ideas, but the courage that one has to bet on his ideas, to take a calculated risk—and to act.

Maxwell Maltz

It is not enough to fight. It is the spirit which we bring to the fight that decides the issue. It's morale that wins the victory.

George C. Marshall

Impossible is a word found only in a fool's dictionary.

Napoleon

Life shrinks or expands in proportion to one's courage.

Anais Nin

I don't measure a man's success by how high he climbs but how high he bounces when he hits bottom.

General George S. Patton

Anyone in a position of leadership who won't go up to his boss and say "I don't agree" is not a leader.

Colin Powell

A leader, once convinced a particular course of action is the right one, must have the determination to stick with it and be undaunted when the going gets rough.

Ronald Reagan

I know it's hard when you're up to your armpits in alligators to remember you came here to drain the swamp.

Ronald Reagan

You've got to go out on a limb sometimes because that's where the fruit is.

Will Rogers

You gain strength, courage and confidence by every experience in which you really stop to look fear in the face. You must do the thing you think you cannot do.

Eleanor Roosevelt

Far better it is to dare mighty things, to win glorious triumphs, even though checkered by failure, than to take rank with those poor spirits who neither enjoy nor suffer much, because they live in the gray twilight that knows neither victory nor defeat.

Theodore Roosevelt

The only man who never makes a mistake is the man who never does anything.

Theodore Roosevelt

A frightened captain makes a frightened crew.

Lister Sinclair

Anyone can hold the helm when the sea is calm.

Publius Syrus

Men make history, and not the other way around. In periods where there is no leadership, society stands still. Progress occurs when courageous, skillful leaders seize the opportunity to change things for the better.

Harry S. Truman

Courage is resistance to fear, mastery of fear—not absence of fear.

Mark Twain

If you stand up and be counted, from time to time you may get yourself knocked down. But remember this: A man flattened by an opponent can get up again. A man flattened by conformity stays down for good.

Thomas J. Watson, Jr.

Chapter 7

Empowerment

Empowerment

Tasks must be delegated without responsibilities being abdicated.

Anonymous

It takes leaders to grow other leaders.

Ray Blunt

The greatness of a leader is measured by the achievements of the led. This is the ultimate test of his effectiveness.

General Omar Bradley

No man will make a great leader who wants to do it all himself or to get all the credit for doing it.

Andrew Carnegie

The best leader brings out the best of those he has stewardship over.

J. Richard Clarke

Any organization will be only as successful as those at the bottom are willing to make it.

General Bill Creech

The greatest good you can do for another is not just share your riches, but reveal to them their own.

Benjamin Disraeli

Probably my best quality as a coach is that I ask a lot of challenging questions and let the person come up with the answer.

Phil Dixon

No executive has ever suffered because his subordinates were strong and effective.

Peter Drucker

Leadership is not magnetic personality—that can just as well be a glib tongue. It is not "making friends and influencing people"—that is flattery. Leadership is lifting a person's vision to high sights, the raising of a person's performance to a higher standard, the building of a personality beyond its normal limitations.

Peter Drucker

Managers should focus on people's strengths instead of their weaknesses. Rather than dwell on the areas where a worker is weak, find out what he does well, determine the context in which he is able to exercise his positive capabilities—and let him do it. Make his shortcomings irrelevant. The function of an organization is to make human strength productive—and this is accomplished by building on people's assets, not by bemoaning their limitations.

Peter Drucker

The growth and development of people is the highest calling of leadership.

Harvey S. Firestone

The more you establish parameters and encourage people to take initiatives within those boundaries, the more you multiply your own effectiveness by the effectiveness of other people.

Robert Hass

The rung of a ladder was never meant to rest upon, but only to hold a man's foot long enough to enable him to put the other somewhat higher.

Thomas Huxley

I've always felt that a manager has achieved a great deal when he's able to motivate one other person. When it comes to making the place run, motivation is everything. You might be able to do the work of two people, but you can't be two people. Instead, you have to inspire the next guy down the line and get him to inspire his people.

Lee Iacocca

When people feel trusted, they'll do almost anything under the sun not to disappoint the person who gave them the gift of trust.

Rob LeBow

To empower well—to help others grow as leaders—is becoming a prime attribute in defining the leader of the 21st Century.

Myles Martel

The art of choosing men is not nearly so difficult as the art of enabling those one has chosen to attain their full worth.

Napoleon

When I give a minister an order, I leave it to him to find [the] means to carry it out.

Napoleon

Don't tell people how to do things, tell them what to do and let them surprise you with their results.

General George S. Patton

Leaders don't create followers, they create more leaders.

Tom Peters

Leadership should be more participative than directive, more enabling than performing.

Mary D. Poole

The best executive is the one who has sense enough to pick good men to do what he wants done, and self-restraint to keep from meddling with them while they do it.

Theodore Roosevelt

It is the nature of a man to rise to greatness if greatness is expected of him.

John Steinbeck

To lead people, walk beside them . . . As for the best leaders, the people do not notice their existence. The next best, the people honor and praise. The next, the people fear; and the next, the people hate. When the best leader's work is done the people say, "We did it ourselves."

Lao Tzu

Treat people as if they were what they ought to be and you help them to become what they are capable of being.

Johann Wolfgang Von Goethe

A true teacher is not the one with the most knowledge, but one who causes the most others to have knowledge. A true leader is not the one with the most followers, but one who creates the most leaders. A true king is not the one with the most subjects, but one who leads the most to royalty.

Neal Donald Walsch

Outstanding leaders go out of the way to boost the self-esteem of their personnel. If people believe in themselves, it's amazing what they can accomplish.

Sam Walton

There are two ways of exerting one's strength: one is pushing down, the other is pulling up.

Booker T. Washington

If GE had to rely on Jack Welch for all ideas, this place would sink in about an hour. I just believed that we were going to have to be far more competitive. The only way to be more competitive was to engage every mind in the organization. You couldn't have anybody on the sidelines.

Jack Welch

Chapter 8

Goodwill

GOODWILL

If we do not lay out ourselves in the service of mankind, whom should we serve?

Abigail Adams

We make a living by what we get; we make a life by what we give.

Winston Churchill

Do not hold the delusion that your advancement is accomplished by crushing others.

Cicero

Always treat your employees exactly as you want them to treat your best customers.

Stephen Covey

When I was young, I admired clever people. Now that I am old, I admire kind people.

Rabbi Abraham Joshua Heschel

I am certain that after the dust of centuries has passed over our cities, we, too, will be remembered not for victories or defeats in battle or politics, but for our contribution to the human spirit.

John F. Kennedy

A leader's impact and fate hinges on the people's confidence that his goodwill toward them far exceeds his self-interest.

Myles Martel

When you come to the table with the attitude of helping and serving, you immediately compound the influence, effectiveness and results of everyone involved.

John C. Maxwell

People don't care how much you know—until they know how much you care.

John C. Maxwell

Your ability to get people to follow you up the hill into gunfire, or into the next Net meltdown, is based on your ability to convince them that you have their best interests at heart.

Dave McCormick

A leader who does not hesitate before he sends his nation into battle is not fit to be a leader.

Golda Meir

No man is great enough or wise enough for any of us to surrender our destiny to. The only way in which anyone can lead us is to restore to us the belief in our own guidance.

Henry Miller

I expect to pass through life but once. If, therefore, there be any kindness I can show, or any good thing I can do for any fellow being, let me do it now . . . as I shall not pass this way again.

William Penn

Leaders focus on the soft stuff. People. Values. Character. Commitment. A cause. All of the stuff that was supposed to be too goo-goo to count in business. Yet, it's the stuff that real leaders take care of first. And forever. That's why leadership is an art, not a science.

Tom Peters

Be kind, for everyone you meet is fighting a hard battle.

Plato

Leadership is all about people. It is not about organizations. It is not about plans. It is not about strategies. It is all about people—motivating people to get the job done. You have to be people-centered.

Colin Powell

A reflective reading of history will show that no man ever rose to military greatness who could not convince his troops that he put them first, above all else.

General Maxwell Taylor

Kind words can be short and easy to speak, but their echoes are truly endless.

Mother Theresa

There is no cause half so sacred as the cause of a people. There is no idea so uplifting as the idea of the service of humanity.

Woodrow Wilson

You cannot live a perfect day without doing something for someone who will never be able to repay you.

John Wooden

Chapter 9

Persuasion & Influence

PERSUASION AND INFLUENCE

The key to successful leadership today is influence, not authority.

Kenneth Blanchard

Woodrow Wilson called for leaders who, by boldly interpreting the nation's conscience, could lift a people out of their everyday selves. That people can be lifted into their better selves is the secret of transforming leadership.

James MacGregor Burns

Speech that leads not to action, still more that hinders it, is a nuisance on the earth.

Thomas Carlyle

In the face of leadership flaws, too many people assume cynical perspectives, rather than do the hard work of building relationships in which they can have more positive influence.

Ira Chaleff

Never hold any one by the button, or the hand, in order to be heard out; for if people are unwilling to hear you, you had better hold your tongue than them.

Lord Chesterfield

It was the nation and the race dwelling all round the globe that had the lion's heart. I had the luck to be called upon to give the roar.

Winston Churchill

We must not, in trying to think about how we can make a big difference, ignore the small daily differences we can make which, over time, add up to big differences that we often cannot foresee.

Marion Wright Edelman

When people are the least sure, they are often most dogmatic.

John Kenneth Galbraith

I suppose that leadership at one time meant muscle; but today it means getting along with the people.

Indira Gandhi

Let no man imagine that he has no influence. Whoever he may be, and wherever he may be placed, the man who thinks becomes a light and a power.

Henry George

Much of your ability to get people to do what they have to do is going to depend on what they perceive when they look at you and listen to you. They need to see someone who is stronger than they are, but human, too.

Rudolph W. Giuliani

Empathy is crucial for wielding influence; it is difficult to have a positive impact on others without first sensing how they feel and understanding their position. People who are poor at reading emotional cues and inept at social interactions are very poor at influence. The first step in influence is building rapport.

Daniel Goleman

That is what leadership is all about: staking your ground ahead of where opinion is and convincing people, not simply following the popular opinion of the moment.

Doris Kearns Goodwin

Remember the difference between a boss and a leader; a boss says "Go!"—a leader says "Let's Go!"

E.M. Kelly

A genuine leader is not a searcher for consensus but a molder of consensus.

Martin Luther King, Jr.

There's nothing more demoralizing than a leader who can't clearly articulate why we're doing what we're doing.

James Kouzes and Barry Posner

Much of Winston Churchill's strength as a war leader derived from this very habit of myth-making, of surrounding even the ordinary and the humdrum with enchantment. Like Shakespeare's Glendower, he could "call the sprits from the vasty deep"—and the British believed in them.

Ronald Lewin

Leadership is based on a spiritual quality; the power to inspire others to follow.

Vince Lombardi

A leader's role as a communicator is to persuade—to influence attitudes and behavior. To merely inform or convey information without a point of view squanders the leader's opportunity to influence others to align with his goals and vision.

Myles Martel

Motivation cannot be merely outsourced to a motivational speaker. Every leader must find within himself an authentic voice to motivate and then use it to his best advantage.

Myles Martel

Of all the fine leaders I've had to privilege to advise, the one communication trait of theirs that has impressed me the most is their ability to listen.

Myles Martel

Listening well competes impressively with words in communicating interest, respect, composure, caring, class, plus a host of other leadership traits.

Myles Martel

Communication is the linchpin of leadership, the main tool the leader possesses to define, advance and sustain his leadership goals.

Myles Martel

When a leader risks losing his composure, he must be aware that his obligation to "logo"—the organization or group he represents—must always take precedence over his ego. Hence, our admonition, "logo, not ego!"

Myles Martel

Nothing is more critical to the art of persuasion than pure unadulterated truth.

Myles Martel

Before you try to convince anyone else, be sure you are convinced, and if you cannot convince yourself, drop the subject.

John H. Patterson

Now if you are going to win any battle you have to do one thing. You have to make the mind run the body. Never let the body tell the mind what to do. The body will always give up. It is always tired morning, noon and night. But the body is never tired if the mind in not tired. When you were younger the mind could make you dance all night, and the body was never tired . . . You've always got to make the mind take over and keep going.

General George S. Patton

The leader must know, must know that he knows, and must be able to make it abundantly clear to those about him that he knows.

Clarence B. Randall

The leader holds his position purely because he is able to appeal to the conscience and to the reason of those who support him, and the boss holds his position because he appeals to fear of punishment and hope of reward.
The leader works in the open, and the boss in covert. The leader leads, and the boss drives.

Theodore Roosevelt

When met with opposition, even if it should be from your husband or your children, endeavor to overcome it by argument and not by authority, for a victory dependent on authority is unreal and illusory.

Bertrand Russell

Example is not the main thing in influencing others. It is the only thing.

Albert Schweitzer

Talkativeness is one thing, speaking well another.

Sophocles

Keep your fears to yourself, but share your inspiration with others.

Robert Louis Stevenson

Nothing serves a leader better than a knack for narrative. Stories anoint role models, impart values, and show how to execute indescribably complex tasks.

Thomas A. Stewart

A leader may symbolize and express what is best in people, like Pericles, or what is worst, like Hitler, but he cannot successfully express what is only in his heart and not in theirs.

Charles Yost

Chapter 10

Preparedness

Preparedness

We can't cross a bridge until we come to it, but I always like to lay down a pontoon ahead of time.

Bernard M. Baruch

If you're tired or fatigued, there is a reasonable chance that your troops are also. Maybe you both need a break. In years past, the mentality in pro football was that a team will outwork and out-tough its opponents. This concept has proven to be naïve. In the NFL, everyone works hard and is tough. To think otherwise is to set yourself up for defeat. What has evolved in the league is the realization that teams should focus on the concept of working more intelligently in order to get their players to the game healthy and fresh. This process must be monitored and gauged by leadership, which itself must also be healthy and fresh for battle.

Brian Billick

Dig a well before you are thirsty.

Chinese Proverb

It is important when you haven't got any ammunition to have a butt on your rifle.

Winston Churchill

Hope for the best, but prepare for the worst.

English Proverb

A community is like a ship; everyone ought to be prepared to take the helm.

Henrik Ibsen

Never wait for trouble.

Charles "Chuck" Yeager

Chapter 11

Self-Awareness & Self-Respect

Self-Awareness and Self-Respect

I have an everyday religion that works for me. Love yourself first and everything else falls into line. You really have to love yourself to get anything done in this world.

Lucille Ball

Nothing splendid has ever been achieved except by those who dared believe that something inside them was superior to circumstance.

Bruce Barton

One of the worst things we do in corporate America is not tell people what we think of them.

Lawrence Bossidy

We are what we believe we are.

Benjamin N. Cardozo

If you want to be respected by others, the great thing is to respect yourself. Only by that, only by self-respect will you compel others to respect you.

Fyodor Dostoevsky

It's never too late to be who you might have been.

George Eliot

Keeping score of old scores and scars, getting even and one-upping, always make you less than you are.

Malcom Forbes

Because emotions are so contagious—especially from leaders to others in the group—leaders' first tasks are the emotional equivalent of good hygiene: getting their own emotions in hand.

Daniel Goleman, Richard Boyatzis, Annie McKee

... you must have a self you respect ... Winston Churchill exemplified integrity and respect in the face of opposition. Churchill was attending an official ceremony. Several rows behind him two gentlemen began whispering, "That's Winston Churchill." "They say he is getting senile." "They say he should step aside and leave the running of the nation to younger, more dynamic, and capable men." Churchill sat facing forward, but when the ceremony was over, he stopped by the row where the men were seated. He leaned forward and said, "Gentlemen, they also say he is deaf!"

Barbara Hatcher

We are taught you must blame your father, your sisters, your brothers, the school, the teachers—you can blame anyone, but never blame yourself. It's never your fault. But it's ALWAYS your fault, because if you wanted to change, you're the one who has got to change. It's as simple as that, isn't it?

Katherine Hepburn

Ability is what you're capable of doing. Motivation determines what you do. Attitude determines how well you do it.

Lou Holtz

The greatest discovery of my generation is that man can alter his life simply by altering his attitude of mind.

William James

I have three precious things which I hold fast and prize. The first is gentleness; the second is frugality; the third is humility, which keeps me from putting myself before others. Be gentle and you can be bold; be frugal and you can be liberal; avoid putting yourself before others and you can become a leader among men.

Lao Tzu

I cannot trust a man to control others who cannot control himself.

Robert E. Lee

Self-image sets the boundaries of individual accomplishment.

Maxwell Maltz

To lead well, a leader must be solidly self-aware. To lead better, a leader should be open to feedback. To lead optimally, a leader should encourage feedback and be willing to act on it.

Myles Martel

We cannot lead others well unless we first lead ourselves well.

Myles Martel

Faith in oneself . . . is the best and safest course.

Michelangelo

The thing that is really hard, and really amazing, is giving up on being perfect and beginning the work of becoming yourself.

Anna Quindlen

Learn to value yourself, which means: to fight for your happiness.

Ayn Rand

No one can make you feel inferior without your consent.

Eleanor Roosevelt

Let him that would move the world, first move himself.

Socrates

Many people have ideas on how others should change; few people have ideas on how they should change.

Tolstoy

You can begin the process of eliminating negative emotions by simply refusing to justify them.

Brian Tracy

Outstanding leaders go out of their way to boost the self-esteem of their personnel. If people believe in themselves, it's amazing what they can accomplish.

Sam Walton

When a man realizes his littleness, his greatness can appear.

H.G. Wells

Do not let what you cannot do interfere with what you can do.

John Wooden

Do not make yourself low; people will tread on your head.

Yiddish Proverb

Chapter 12

Teamwork

Teamwork

One man can be a crucial ingredient on a team, but one man cannot make a team.

Kareem Abdul-Jabbar

None of us is as smart as all of us.

Ken Blanchard

Teamwork is the ability to work together toward a common vision. It is the fuel that allows common people to attain uncommon results.

Andrew Carnegie

The leaders who work most effectively, it seems to me, never say "I". And that's not because they have trained themselves not to say "I". They don't think "I". They think "we"; they think "team." They understand their job to be to make the team function. They accept responsibility and don't sidestep it, but "we" gets the credit . . . This is what creates trust, what enables you to get the task done.

Peter Drucker

Teamwork is neither "good" nor "desirable." It is a fact. Wherever people work together or play together they do so as a team. Which team to use for what purpose is a crucial, difficult and risky decision that is even harder to unmake. Managements have yet to learn how to make it.

Peter Drucker

No member of a crew is praised for the rugged individuality of his rowing.

Ralph Waldo Emerson

Coming together is a beginning. Keeping together is progress. Working together is success.

Henry Ford

Talent wins games, but teamwork and intelligence win championships.

Michael Jordan

Alone we can do so little; together we can do so much.

Helen Keller

Individual commitment to a group effort—that is what makes a team work, a company work, a society work, a civilization work.

Vince Lombardi

There's nothing greater in the world than when somebody on the team does something good, and everybody gathers around to pat him on the back.

Billy Martin

When you cease to make a contribution you begin to die.

Eleanor Roosevelt

The way a team plays as a whole determines its success. You may have the greatest bunch of individual stars in the world, but if they don't play together, the club won't be worth a dime.

Babe Ruth

A group becomes a team when each member is sure enough of himself and his contribution to praise the skills of others.

Norman Shidle

Finding good players is easy. Getting them to play as a team is another story.

Casey Stengel

When he took time to help the man up the mountain, lo, he scaled it himself.

Tibetan Proverb

If a team is to reach its potential, each player must be willing to subordinate his personal goals to the good of the team.

Bud Wilkinson

I not only use all the brains I have, but all I can borrow.

Woodrow Wilson

Chapter 13

Vision

Vision

Vision without action is daydreaming, but action without vision is just random activity.

Joel Barkers

The great difference between the real leader and the pretender is that the one sees into the future, while the other regards only the present; the one lives by the day, and acts upon expediency; the other acts on enduring principles and for the immortality.

Edmund Burke

The ultimate test of practical leadership is the realization of intended, real change that meets people's enduring needs.

James MacGregor Burns

Goal setting is the strongest force for human motivation. Set a goal and make it come true.

Jack Canfield and Mark Victor Hansen

If you can dream it, you can do it.

Walt Disney

The best way to predict the future is to create it.

Peter Drucker

Leadership is the special quality which enables people to stand up and pull the rest of us over the horizon.

James L. Fisher

To accomplish great things, we must not only act but also dream, not only plan, but also believe.

Anatole France

Leadership can be thought of as a capacity to define oneself to others in a way that clarifies and expands a vision of the future.

Edwin H. Friedman

We must become the change we want to see.

Mahatma Gandhi

[Leaders] can express the values that hold the society together. Most important, they can conceive and articulate goals that lift people out of their petty preoccupations, carry them above the conflicts that tear a society apart, and unite them in the pursuit of objectives worthy of their best efforts.

John W. Gardner

The ability to sense how others feel and to understand their perspectives means that a leader can articulate a truly inspirational vision. A leader who misreads people, on the other hand, simply can't inspire them.

Daniel Goleman, Richard Boyatzis, Annie McKee

The very essence of leadership is that you have to have vision. You can't blow an uncertain trumpet.

Theodore M. Hesburgh

We need men who can dream of things that never were.

John F. Kennedy

Leaders must invoke an alchemy of great vision.

Henry Kissinger

Leaders establish the vision for the future and set the strategy for getting there.

John P. Kotter

You have to know one big thing and stick with it . . . The leaders who had one very big idea and one very big commitment. This permitted them to create something. Those are the ones who leave a legacy.

Irving Kristol

Successful leaders see the opportunities in every difficulty rather than the difficulty in every opportunity.

Reed Markham

If I have seen farther than others, it is because I was standing on the shoulder of giants.

Sir Isaac Newton

Leadership is more than a technique, though techniques are necessary. In a sense, management is prose; leadership is poetry . . . The manager thinks of today and tomorrow. The leader must think of the day after tomorrow. A manager represents a process. The leader represents a direction of history.

Richard M. Nixon

Optimism is a force multiplier.

Colin Powell

Where there is no vision, the people perish.

Proverbs 29:18

The challenge of statesmanship is to have the vision to dream of a better, safer world and the courage, persistence, and patience to turn that dream into reality.

Ronald Reagan

. . . there is no limit to what a man can do or where he can go if he doesn't mind who gets the credit.

Ronald Reagan

We in government should learn to look at our country with the eyes of the entrepreneur, seeing possibilities where others see only problems.

Ronald Reagan

You see things; and you say, "Why?" But I dream things that never were; and I say, "Why not?"

George Bernard Shaw

Do not follow where the path may lead. Go instead where there is no path and leave a trail.

Muriel Strode

You are not here merely to make a living. You are here to enable the world to live more amply, with greater vision, and with a finer spirit of hope and achievement. You are here to enrich the world.

Woodrow Wilson

Just because a man lacks the use of his eyes doesn't mean he lacks vision.

Stevie Wonder

When all is said and done, there is so much left to say and do.

Myles Martel

Special Appreciation

2005 marked he 25th anniversary of our practice. Referrals have been the foundation of the success Martel and Associates has enjoyed throughout our history. Referrals from the following persons have been instrumental in building and reinforcing our foundation, including our reputation.

John Adams	George Butler*	Mitch Daniels
Aram Aghazarian	Marie Butz	Kathleen Davis
Margaret Alden	Jim Cavanaugh	Matt Davis
Griffin Allen	Marie Chinnici	Livio DeSimone
John Allison	Tom Churchwell	Fred DiBona*
Coleman Andrews	Richard Collins	Tobey Dichter
Richard Anthony	Vic Coppola	Richard Evans
Mike Bailey	Lauren Cotter-Brobson	Blaine Fabian
John Ballantyne		Mike Falco
Buddy Barfield	Lucie Cousineau	Julie Fasone-Holder
Herb Barness*	Paul Critchlow	Mark Fenner
Larry Beaser	Bernie Cronin	Brain Ferguson
Barry Berkowitz	Bill Crouse	Regis Filtz*
George Biltz	Paul Curcio	Charlie Fisher
George Bothwell	Marc Cutis	Steve Gadomski
Vince Breglio	Tom D'Ambra	Faith Goldstein
David Brightbill	Hemant Dandekar	Rosemarie Greco
Al Butkus	Frank Daniel	Rick Green

Ron Green
Carlos Guimaraes
Harriet Hankin
Phil Harris
Bill Hecht
Marc Holtzman
George Horner
Brian Hull
Tod Hullin
Susan Hullin
Jon Humphreys
Len Jacobs
Julie Johnson
Preston Johnson
Robert Jubilier
Wally Judd
Marci Kaminsky
Andreas Karl
Graham King
Jeane Kirkpatrick
Sherry Knight
Dave Komansky
Romeo Kreinberg
Charles Kresge
Kathy Lamensdorf
Robert Laskowski
Frank Lavelle
Martha Lawson
Ron Lehrer
Steve Linehan
John Littlechild
Andrew Liveris
Margaret Llamas
Mike Long
Frank Luijckx
James Macaleer
Jim Malott
Amy Margolis
Brian Mattes

Dan McCarthy
Bob McCormack
Sam McCullough
Kevin McElgunn
Sally McElwreath
Dennis McKeever
John McKinley
Kirk Michael
Emmy Miller
Chris Mirabelli
Rich Monaghan
Michelle Morris
Richard Nelson
David Osterhout
Harvey Padewar
Sherry Pailet
Chris Pappas
Ed Parrish
Jack Pelton
Gary Perlin
Kathy Phillips
Brenna Quinn
Joanne Raphael
Ed Rudnic
Charles Rockey
Carol Rosenbaum
Arthur Rosenberg
Donald Rumsfeld
Frank Ryan
Lisa Salamon
Michelle Schiavoni
Patti Seif
Steve Shallcross
Paul Shapiro
Steve Shihadeh
Gary Slack
Kip Smith
Thym Smith
Shanin Specter

Rob Spurling
Bill Stavropolous
Kurt Swogger
Robert Thompson
John Tognino
Matt Townley
Tony Torres
Howard Ungerleider
Frank Ursomarso
John Venardos
Gary Veurink
Jim Walters
Karol Wasylyshyn
Henry Wendt
Joe Westner
Gaylon White
Roger Whyte
Jim Wiggins
Jim Williams*
Brian Wilson
Bernie Windon*
Linda Wingate
Richard Wirthlin
Damon Womack
David Wright
John Yimoyines

* deceased

For further information regarding Martel & Associates,
please visit our website:
www.martelandassociates.com
or call:
561-868-0300

If you have a quote you would like to add to a future edition of this book, please e-mail it to MMartel@aol.com, citing "New Quotation: Legacies" in the heading. If selected, you will be acknowledged in a footnote and receive a gift from us.

All royalties will be donated to the Ronald Reagan Presidential Library and to charitable relief efforts devoted to natural disasters throughout the world.

Printed in the United States
79571LV00004B/337